SOUND

SCIENCE SECRETS

Jason Cooper

Rourke

Publishing LLC
Vero Beach, Florida 32964

www.rourkepublishing.com

PHOTO CREDITS: © Lynn M. Stone: Cover, pages 4, 10, 15, 17, 21; © Corbis Images: page 7; © Eyewire: title pages, page 12; © U.S.A.F.: pages 8, 13; © Painet, Inc: page 18

Title page: *People can hear you coming if you ring your bike bell.*

Series Editor: Henry Rasof

Cover and interior design by Nicola Stratford

Library of Congress Cataloging-in-Publication Data

Cooper, Jason, 1942-
  Sound / Jason Cooper.
     v. cm. — (Science secrets)
Includes bibliographical references and index.
Contents: Sound everywhere — Sound waves all around us — How we talk — How we hear sounds — High and low sounds — Sound that bounces — "Looking" with sound beams — Radar and sonar — The speed of sound.
  ISBN 1-58952-413-6
  1. Sound—Juvenile literature. [1. Sound.] I. Title. II. Series:
     Cooper, Jason, d 1942- . Science secrets.
QC225.5 .C68 2002
534—dc21
                                          2002015736

Printed in the USA

CG/CG

TABLE OF CONTENTS

SOUND EVERYWHERE

Sound is all around us. Dogs bark. Machines whirr. Phones ring. Everything we hear is sound, and sounds are everywhere.

Sound is caused by **vibrations**. Vibrations are quick movements that go back and forth. Vibrations make invisible movements in the air. These movements are a kind of **energy**, or power. We hear these vibrations as sounds.

Some people, however, have hearing problems or cannot hear at all.

A koala makes sounds because of vibrations.

SOUND WAVES ALL AROUND US

Sound moves in waves. Sound waves are most powerful close to the source. As sound waves move away from their source, they become weaker. Sound waves are **conducted**, or carried, by air. But other substances, such as water, can also conduct sound.

The noise from a boat motor can be heard underwater.

HOW WE TALK

Remember that sound is a vibration. When we talk, the **vocal** organs in our throats make the air vibrate. We use the movements of our tongues and lips to shape the sounds into words. And when animals make noises, the vocal organs in their throats also vibrate.

Lips help shape sounds into words.

HOW WE HEAR SOUNDS

When a wolf howls, sound travels from the vibrations in its throat. The sound waves from the wolf enter our ears. Then the waves reach special organs in our ears. These organs send messages to the part of our brain that hears sound waves.

Most humans can hear well. Some animals, like dogs, bats, and owls, can hear even better. They can hear faint sounds or high-pitched sounds that humans cannot hear.

With people who have a hearing **impairment**, their deafness or hearing loss can have any number of causes. These include disease and also defects in the ear.

Two wolves in a howling contest

Race car engines are very loud.

Ear protection must be worn when working around loud jet engines.

HIGH AND LOW SOUNDS

Some sounds we hear are "high," or high-pitched. A mosquito makes such a sound. This is because the mosquito's wings vibrate rapidly. These vibrations make sound waves. There are so many of these vibrations that the sounds are high-pitched.

On the other hand, some animals make "low," or low-pitched, sounds. The roar of an angry hippo is such a sound. The hippo's vocal organs make few vibrations, so the sounds are low-pitched.

An angry, roaring hippo

SOUND THAT BOUNCES

If you shout into a tunnel or mountain valley, your voice seems to repeat itself. This is known as an **echo**. Say a word, and the word bounces back to you.

This is because sound "bounces." You hear an echo of your voice because a hard surface bounces the sound waves back to you. Your voice rebounds in only a short time. Sometimes one shout creates many echoes.

An echo bounces back across a mountain valley.

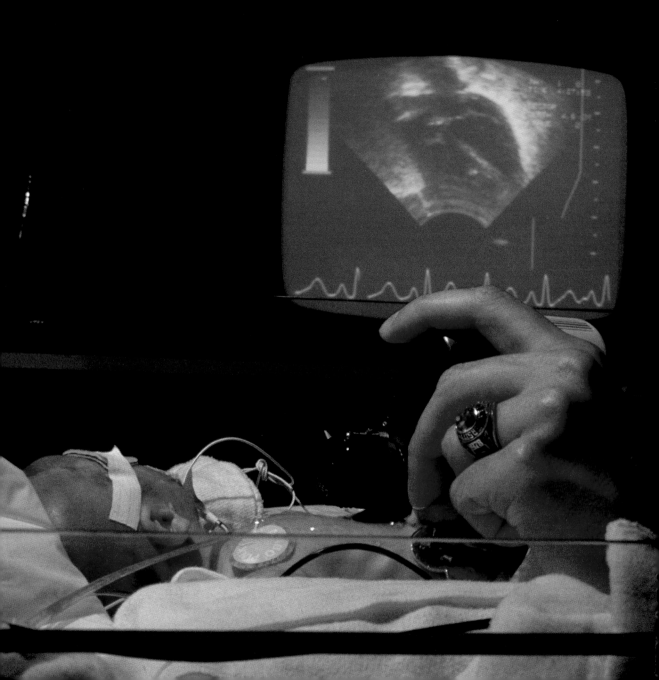

"LOOKING" WITH SOUND BEAMS

Special, narrow beams of sound are used to look at objects that we cannot see. The beam of sound may travel a long way or just a few inches.

A beam that hits an object bounces a sound wave back, just like an echo. We cannot hear the sounds, but special instruments can detect them.

These waves can even travel through our skin. Doctors use sound waves to look inside a patient's body. They then make a picture of what they bounce off. Inside the body, for example, they may bounce off the heart. The process is called **ultrasound**.

An ultrasound machine uses sound waves to create a picture.

RADAR AND SONAR

Radar and **sonar** use sound and special instruments to locate objects. The information shows up on a screen. Looking at a radar screen can tell us where a distant airplane or ship is. Bats use their own radar system to hunt for insects.

A sonar screen works with underwater sound waves. It can locate certain fish and even submarines. Dolphins and porpoises use built-in sonar to locate fish. They also use it to communicate with other dolphins and porpoises.

Porpoises have "built-in" sonar.

THE SPEED OF SOUND

Sound moves quickly. But it is not nearly as fast as the speed of light. Because of this, you may see lightning in the sky before you hear the boom of thunder.

When you shout, your voice travels quickly through air. Underwater, sound waves travel even more quickly. This is because some substances carry sound better than others.

GLOSSARY

conducted (kuhn DUCK ted) — carried along a pathway of some kind

echo (EH ko) — a sound repeated when it bounces off a surface back toward its maker

energy (EN er jee) — power; the ability to work

impairment (im PARE munt) — disability

radar (RAY dar) — a system in which sound wave echoes are used to locate objects in the air

sonar (SOH nar) — a system in which sound waves are used to locate objects under the water

ultrasound (UHL trah souhnd) — a machine that makes a picture of sound waves; usually used by doctors to discover problems in the human body

vibrations (vie BRAY shunz) — rapid, back-and-forth motions

vocal (VO kuhl) — having to do with the voice

Index

Further Reading

Cobb, Vicki. *Bangs and Twangs: Science Fun with Sound*. Millbrook, 2000.
Glover, David. *The Super Science Book of Sound*. New York: Thomson Learning, 1994.
The Magic School Bus in the Haunted Museum: A Book about Sound. New York: Scholastic, 1999.   .

Websites To Visit

www.sfskids.org/templates/splash.asp
www.science-tech.nmstc.ca/english/schoolzone/Info_Sound.cfm
library.thinkquest.org/11924/sound.html/

About The Author

Jason Cooper has written several children's book series about a variety of topics for Rourke Publishing, including *Eye to Eye with Big Cats* and *Money Power*. Cooper travels widely to gather information for his books.